SPIRITUAL CHARACTER

By the same author:
Battle for Israel
The Uniqueness of Israel
Watch and Pray

Spiritual Character

LANCE LAMBERT

KINGSWAY PUBLICATIONS
EASTBOURNE

Original transcript published by Christian Tape Ministry,
Richmond, Virginia.

This edition first published 1995

ISBN 0 85476 559 X

Designed and produced by
Bookprint Creative Services
P.O. Box 827, BN21 3YJ, England for
KINGSWAY PUBLICATIONS LTD
Lottbridge Drove, Eastbourne, E. Sussex BN23 6NT.
Printed in Great Britain.

Contents

1
Samuel

1

Samuel

MINISTRY TO THE LORD

In this book I will be looking at four characters in the Old Testament. The qualities exemplified in these four figures, either positively or negatively, are those the Lord looks for in us in the building of his house, in the fulfilling of the purpose of God and in any recovery work. Together they point to the kind of spiritual character that God requires if the kingdom of God is going to be established. We are looking at Samuel, Saul, David and Solomon.

Samuel is one of the greatest characters in the Bible. In Jewish tradition, particularly, Samuel is next only to Moses and Elijah, and his story is recognised as one of the great turning points in the purpose of God. Samuel was destined by God to bring in the true king, the one who would build the house of the Lord. Here is a remarkable man standing at the turning point in history, and we would do well to learn from him. He gave God such a place in his life that God was able to fulfil his purposes through him.

Character is the all-important matter. There can be no bringing in of the kingdom of God, no establishing of the throne, the authority and the rule of God in our lives or in our life together unless there is real spiritual character. We are living in days when an enormous

9

emphasis is being placed on outward things. Don't misunderstand me: we need signs and wonders; we need God to break into our circumstances, into our lives, into our communities, into our nations. We need the evidence of the Lord among us, evidence for the truth of the gospel that we preach. But we are living in days when, very sadly, an emphasis is being put upon signs and wonders and the absolute and vital need for spiritual character is being overlooked. In the end, signs and wonders will pass away and miracles will cease. All those outward things are temporary and transient. But the spiritual character that the Holy Spirit produces in our lives, through situations in our families, in our businesses, in our fellowship together as God's people—that is for ever. That is why the worker is far more important to God than the work he does. God will take unbelievable pains with a worker of his to equip him for service. And I do not mean just down here either; I mean eternal service. Sometimes God may take a servant of his out of the work and out of the ministry and put him on one side, maybe for years, in order to do a work in that person that no one sees. We would like to have that person on the platform or in the pulpit, but for God, spiritual character is far more important.

Spiritual character is the nature of the Lord Jesus and the life of the Lord Jesus made real in us. But there is a price to pay. And that is the big problem, because it is there that we all tend to falter and hesitate. When we talk about spiritual character as we see it in Samuel, in David, and in Solomon, or as we see it lacking in Saul, then we are coming face to face with the heart of the matter. We are living in the shadow of the coming kingdom. We are on the very threshold of the public appearance of the kingdom of God with our Lord Jesus. Actually, if we are born again, then this kingdom of God has already come to us. We have entered the kingdom by a new birth. But the question remains: can God do in us what is required to produce in us genuine, eternal, Christ-like character that alone will be able to reign with the Lord Jesus in his kingdom? That is my burden for these times.

Unconditionally given

If we are going to be involved in bringing in the kingdom, if we are going to reign in that kingdom, if we are going to have a part in the building of God's house and the fulfilment of his purpose, then the first thing is this: we have to be *unconditionally* given to the Lord. There are no half measures, no percentages. It is not sixty per cent given to the Lord, eighty per cent given to the Lord, ninety per cent given to the Lord. It is absolute and unconditional.

For us to reach God's end, everything necessary has been given. All the grace of God is available to you and me to bring us from where we are now to completion in the Lord. No matter what the obstacles or problems, no matter how great Satan might be, no matter if the whole of our circumstances are filled with demons; the grace of God has been made available to us to bring us from sinner to saint, to bring us from ugly people to being absolutely conformed to the image of God's Son, to bring us from babyhood to full maturity in the Lord. All the grace and power of God's Holy Spirit, the power in the resurrection of the Lord Jesus is made available to us to achieve his purposes.

Why is it then that we do not avail ourselves of this

grace and this power? We all have excuses. We may have complex personalities or deep, inbuilt complexes that make it very difficult. We may think we are unique. We think that God can take all the others, but we have inherited something from our backgrounds, our culture, our circumstances, or we have a husband or a wife who is an immovable obstacle, or children who are so difficult, or parents who are such a problem that we cannot fulfil the purposes of the Lord.

What are we talking about? Do we really think that when the Lord saved us, he had no idea what our circumstances would be or what our genetic history was? Does he think, 'Oh, I had no idea when I saved so-and-so that they had such a genetic history. No one showed me their pedigree or what has got into their blood stream. I had no idea they were such difficult people. Really, if I had known this, I would never have saved them in the first place'?

When the Lord saved you, he not only knew you in your mother's womb, he knew your whole genetic history. He knew every single thing that makes up you—your personality, your temperament, your cultural background. He knew all the problems that you would have in your marriage, your business, your career. It is an open book before the Lord and he knew it all before he saved you—before you were even born. And he made available to you grace commensurate with your problems. So if you have unique problems, you have unique grace. If you have unique difficulties, you have unique power available to you. The Lord has not rationed out the same grace to everybody and said, 'Now this is grace.' If you have a very difficult history and very difficult circumstances, you have special grace. Therefore, you have no excuse.

Do not say you cannot go on with the Lord, that you are too difficult for him. What are you talking about? Nothing is too difficult for the Lord, not even you! Even if the enemy is doing a war dance in your circumstances, that will not stop the Lord from bringing you from sinner to saint *if* you will only give yourself unconditionally to him. Our problem is that we only give thirty per cent to the Lord and we expect him to be able to turn us into a saint from a sinner on that thirty per cent. The Lord says that that is not the bargain. 'If I save you by grace, I need you completely. If you will trust me wholly with your life, your circumstances, your business, your family, then I will give to you all the grace and power in practical terms to bring you from where you are to where I want you to be.' This is the wonderful lesson we learn from the life of Samuel.

> And she was in bitterness of soul, and prayed unto the Lord, and wept sore. And she vowed a vow, and said, O Lord of hosts, if thou wilt indeed look on the affliction of thine handmaid, and remember me, and not forget thine handmaid, but wilt give unto thine handmaid a man child, then I will give him unto the Lord all the days of his life, and there shall no razor come upon his head (1 Samuel 1:10–11).

Dear Hannah, she had no child. The one great passion in her life was to have a child. And because they had tried and tried to have a child and had never been able to have one, it was only natural for her to think that if the Lord gave her one child it would be her only child. Peninnah had many children. It would have been only

13

natural for Hannah to say to God, 'She has so many. You can have one of hers, Lord—she will still have all the others.' But Hannah was not like that. She said, 'If you give me one child, I will give him back to you all the days of his life.'

The Scripture does not actually record it, but we can be pretty sure that Hannah instructed Samuel from the earliest days that he was for the Lord. Samuel could have rebelled, but we do not get even a breath of suspicion anywhere in the record that Samuel rebelled. We find that when he was weaned and taken up to the house of the Lord, he went, seemingly quite happily. It is an amazing story.

Hannah called her boy in Hebrew *Shemuel*, which means 'the name of the Lord'. Isn't that beautiful? It is as if she were saying: 'This one is yours. He is named with the name of the Lord. He belongs to the Lord all the days of his life, not sixty per cent, not eighty per cent, not ninety per cent, but one hundred per cent for the Lord.' It is so simple. If you and I are going to be involved in the kingdom in the days to come, if we are going to build the house of God and see the purpose of God fulfilled, we have to be unconditionally given to the Lord all the days of our lives.

So why do we have such problems on this issue?

None of us wants to go to hell, and I think it is also true that none of us wants a wasted life. Suppose I were to ask you, 'Do you want to be like the Lord Jesus?' If you really know him and were absolutely honest, you would say, 'I do.' Suppose I were to ask you, 'Do you really want to fulfil the Lord's purposes for your life?' I think you would say to me, 'I do.' So why do we resist committing ourselves to the Lord? What is wrong with us? I have known so many thirty per cent, sixty per cent, and eighty per cent committed Christians. I have been among them all my life, and I have not found any of them happy. They are all neurotic and restless because they have one foot in the world and one foot in the kingdom; one foot in self and one foot in Christ. They do not know where they are. They are double-minded and unstable in all their ways, and they have a bad conscience all the time. They feel they should really be moving with the Lord, but they cannot. They feel that they should be doing exploits for God, but they cannot. There is a civil war going on inside them.

But I have also been privileged to know those who have given themselves unconditionally to the Lord Jesus one hundred per cent, with all their weaknesses and failings, and with all their sins. In these people I have seen peace and joy and life more abundant, and laughter and joy unspeakable and full of glory. Now I am not talking about those artificial, pious, stained-glass window saints who have long, drawn faces and dark rings under their eyes and look as if they are from another planet. That is what most people think is a hundred per cent believer—someone who looks as though the blood has been taken out of them, pasty white, anaemic, spineless. Someone who is not human any more.

Maybe that is why we often have this resistance in us. We feel if we let the Lord have his way in our lives, we will become one of those artificial, stained-glass, unreal, pious saints. It is not true; it is absolutely not true. You let the Lord have his way in your life and you will be led from grace to grace. You will discover the power of God in your weakness. In all your failings, you will discover the unbelievable, incredible power of

God to bring you through and to do in you what should be done in your life. This is the first thing to underline in the life of Samuel. He was unconditionally given to the Lord. I wonder if the Lord could say of you, 'Named with my name in reality. That one is mine; not just in position, but in reality.'

Hearing and obeying

Hearing and obeying the Lord is absolutely strategic in the producing of Christian character. No one can have character produced in them, no one can become Christ-like, unless they hear and obey the Lord.

I find this little character Samuel very interesting. He was so young, but when the Lord said, 'Samuel, Samuel,' he said, 'Here am I.' Since he thought it must be Eli calling him, he went to him, but Eli said: 'No, go back to bed. I didn't call you; you are dreaming.'

The boy went back to bed, and again, the Lord said, 'Samuel, Samuel.' Again, he got up and went to Eli. This happened three times. At last Eli perceived that it was the Lord. (Eli was not too good at perceiving the Lord; he thought Hannah was drunk when she was praying in agony. Now here he is again.) At last he recognised who it was and he said, 'Go back, and when the Lord speaks, you say, "Speak Lord, your servant [your bondslave] hears."'

It is interesting that the very first thing the Lord talked about after he gave the Ten Commandments dealt with this matter of a bondslave. If a master has a Hebrew bondslave and that slave does not want to leave when his year of Jubilee or deliverance comes around, the word of God says that the master shall take the servant to the gate and with an awl pierce through his ear (see Exodus 21:1–6). Why would the master pierce the ear with an awl? Wouldn't it just heal up again? This is where it is good to have a little bit of Jewish tradition. This one tells us that the servant had a gold ring put through his ear. Everyone who saw the ring in the ear knew instantly that this was a bondslave who had given himself for ever to his master. He would never go out of his master's house. There, like a wedding ring, was the gold ring in his ear.

The Lord didn't say to the master, 'And you shall take him to your study and put a gold ring on his finger, stamped with your name.' That would have been perfectly sensible to most of us: 'Oh yes, of course, a ring on his finger—this means something. After all, a servant has to use his hands, doesn't he?' What if the Lord said, 'The master shall take him to some place and put a bangle of gold on his ankle'? We would have said: 'Oh, what wonderful typology because a servant always has to walk and do things using his feet.' No: you can have hands that work and feet that walk, but if the master does not have your ear, you are no use.

There is so much Christian service going on today. God's people are full of energy, full of works, full of activity. Many of them are near to a nervous breakdown; they are totally worn out because they are doing things the Lord has never commanded. This is something for all of us to hear. We can think the need is the call, and off we go without listening. We say, 'I have got strong arms, good hands, my fingers are able and dexterous. All these things I can do. I have good strong legs and feet. I can walk.' But the Lord says, 'No matter how strong your arms are, how firm your grasp, how strong your legs, if I do not have your ear, you are no use to me.'

We will never reach the throne of God by simple activity. We will never reach the kingdom or come to reign with Christ by doing things.

In the book of Leviticus, chapters 13–14, we have a description of what leprosy is, whether in the body, in the clothing, or in the house. When it comes to the person who is a leper, however, we read:

> And the priest shall take some of the blood of the trespass offering, and the priest shall put it upon the tip of the right ear of him that is to be cleansed, and upon the thumb of his right hand, and upon the great toe of his right foot. And the priest shall take some of the log of oil, and pour it into the palm of his own left hand: and the priest shall dip his right finger in the oil that is in his left hand, and shall sprinkle of the oil with his finger seven times before the Lord: And of the rest of the oil that is in his hand shall the priest put upon the tip of the right ear of him that is to be cleansed, and upon the thumb of his right hand, and upon the great toe of his right foot (Leviticus 14:14–17).

First the blood is placed on the ear, then on the thumb, then on the toe. First, saved hearing, then saved working, and then saved going. Here is the whole activity of life—but it begins with the ear. It is the Holy Spirit's work to anoint the ear so we can hear the Lord. Not only must we have new ears; we must also use them to listen to the Lord. Here is the lesson of Samuel. Samuel can hear and obey the Lord. 'Speak, Lord, your servant hears.'

When I was young in the Lord I was full of questions and sometimes I would find it difficult if people could not answer me clearly and in a way I could understand.

'I don't understand,' I would say, and I would go on worrying like a dog with a bone. A dear old Swedish aunt always used to say to me, 'Those who do the will of God shall know the doctrine whether it is true' (see John 7:17). In other words, God does not have to reveal anything to you. Only if you are willing to *do* what he reveals to you will he reveal. Why should the Lord cast pearls before swine? We will turn around and rend them with our own stupidity and foolishness. If we are prepared to do the will of God, then the Lord reveals it.

The Lord may speak to us on many different things. It might be about baptism; it might be about losing your reputation; he may ask you to go and apologise to somebody; or to make restitution. Sometimes he may speak to us about worldliness, about not going to the cinema, or not playing sports or something else. What the Lord says to you may not be what he is saying to me. But the point I am making is this: when the Lord speaks to you and you disregard it, he may not speak again.

At the very beginning of Samuel's life, there was a readiness to hear the Lord and to obey him, and this continued right through his life. If you look through the first book of Samuel, you will see how the Lord said, 'Go to such and such a place, and you shall see such and such coming, and you shall do this and this.' First, it was with Saul and then with David. And then it says, 'When the people said this and this, Samuel cried unto the Lord, and the Lord heard him and answered him.' In other words, there was about Samuel a readiness to listen to the Lord and to obey him, and therefore the Lord honoured him.

When we come to the last book of the Bible and to

that great message of the risen, ascended, glorified Messiah in the midst of seven churches, to every church there is the same message: 'He that hath an ear, let him hear what the Spirit says to the churches.' And again in the last chapter of Revelation, we have the same refrain: 'If anyone will hear . . . ' Why do we not hear? If at one time in your life there was a hearing and obeying and now it is all gone, you need to go back to the point where you disregarded the Lord, and listen to him again, because that is the point from which the Lord will take you on.

Ministry to the Lord

There is a third great lesson from the life of Samuel— his ministry was supremely unto the Lord. It is very interesting that right through this account of Samuel's life it says again and again, 'And Samuel ministered unto the Lord.' Now we would say if we looked at Samuel's life, 'And Samuel ministered to the people, to the children of Israel.' But that is not what it says in the scripture:

> And Elkanah went to Ramah to his house. And the child did minister unto the Lord before Eli the priest (1 Samuel 2:11).

> And the child Samuel ministered unto the Lord (1 Samuel 3:1a).

It is not an accident or a coincidence that the Scriptures say that Samuel ministered to the Lord, even before he really came to know him. The Scriptures do not say, 'He ministered to the high priest,' or 'He ministered in the temple or the tabernacle,' or 'He ministered to the people.' It consistently says, 'He ministered to the Lord,' and this reveals to us something about the character of Samuel throughout his life.

We all know what ministry to the world is: that we are called to go out and make disciples of all nations, to preach the gospel in the whole creation, to have a burden for the world and to seek to bring the Lord Jesus to the world. This is ministering to the world. We also know that we are called to minister to one another. But what does it mean to minister to the Lord? That is another dimension of ministry and it is very rare. I do not believe anyone will ever come to the throne of God to rule and reign with Christ who has not learned, in some measure, to minister to the Lord.

Sometimes we can get into a kind of self-perpetuating routine. We get involved in ministry to the world and before we know where we are we are trapped by a kind of perpetual motion. You hardly have to do anything—things just roll on and take you with them. And ministry to the Lord is pushed out and forgotten.

Devotion

The Lord Jesus is a Person, and first and foremost, you and I are to minister to him as a Person. It is perfectly right that we experience him, live by him, feed on him and appropriate his life and fulness and power. But never think of the Lord Jesus as an item, as an *it*, as a life, as a power. He is a Person. Ministry to the Lord Jesus means first and foremost a devotion to him as a Person.

Many years ago I was in a big conference at the Honour Oak centre in London and a certain brother came with a very dramatic message. I remember being startled by the clarity and the authority of this brother's ministry. His message was all to do with feeding on the Lord and experiencing Christ as life. A week or two later I was spending some time with one of the godliest brothers in that company of saints and he asked me, 'What did you think about that message?'

'It was wonderful,' I said. 'I was stunned by it.'

'Yes,' he said, 'but I have a problem. When you speak about Jesus only as life, only as power, only as fulness, as someone or something to experience and appropriate, you cannot worship him. He is inside.'

I could not understand what he meant, so he explained: 'It is a kind of self-worship. You are Christ, therefore you worship inside. You cannot do it. Worship is objective.'

I have thought about it over the years, and I have come to see that many of our problems begin here. We emphasise Christ as life and fulness and power and water and bread and everything else—all of which is right—but we have forgotten that the Lord Jesus is a Person, and we have not worshipped him. Ministry to the Lord is not just feeding on the Lord, it is not just appropriating the Lord as if he is an *it*, a power, as if he is merely instrumental. Ministry to the Lord is falling before him and worshipping him; it is being lost in wonder, love and praise. And you can only do that when you are carried out of yourself. You cannot do it by looking inside. You have to look away.

Ministry to the Lord is absolute and uncompromising devotion to the Person of the Lord. It is like Daniel refusing to eat anything that the Lord had declared unclean even if it cost him his life. It is like the three men who would not bow down to an idol but said, 'We know our God is able to deliver us from the fiery furnace, but if he does not we will not bow down to this idol.' This is an uncompromising devotion to the Person of the Lord Jesus.

Worship

> Wherefore the Lord God of Israel saith, I said indeed that thy house, and the house of thy father, should walk before me for ever: but now the Lord saith, Be it far from me; for them that honour me I will honour, and they that despise me shall be lightly esteemed (1 Samuel 2:30).

Ministry to the Lord is honouring him in everything. It is worship. By that I don't just mean singing a song or saying 'Thank you' for something that God has done. The word worship originally meant acknowledging the worth-ship of the Lord. He is worthy. Some Christians feel they can only really worship, as they call it, when the Lord has done something for them. 'Now I can thank him; now I can worship him.' But to worship the Lord is to see him, his worthiness and his character.

Worship is the most wonderful thing in this world. Men and women were created by God to worship him. I do not know if you realise that, but it is the most fundamental thing about our creation. We were made to worship, and all human beings worship. If they do not worship God, they worship an idol. If they do not worship an idol, they worship another human being. If they do not worship another human being, they worship some sport or some art or something, because every human being has been made in such a way that he or she has to worship. And Jesus put it in the simplest way when he said that God seeks those who will worship him in spirit and in truth (see John 4:23).

It is a wonderful thing when we are so carried out of ourselves in worship and the sense of the Lord's presence that we forget other people, we forget the place, and we are lost in praise and lost in worship. I think I can say without fear of contradiction that once you have really worshipped the Lord you touch something so fulfilling and so deep that you cannot ever be the same again. Why is that? It is because when you really move out of yourself, forget yourself, forget your circumstances and worship the Lord, you are actually fulfilling the thing for which you were created. That is why that deep sense of peace and joy comes into your spirit.

Faithfulness

Samuel is proverbial for his faithfulness. If you remember, he could have easily compromised on so many things, but because of his ministry to the Lord he was absolutely faithful. The Lord said:

> And I will raise me up a faithful priest, that shall do according to that which is in my heart and in my mind: and I will build him a sure house; and he shall walk before mine anointed for ever (1 Samuel 2:35).

What a beautiful picture of Samuel in his ministry to the Lord, faithful in everything that God gave him to do and watching over the work of the Lord.

Intercession

Ministry to the Lord is intercession. Not prayer, but intercession. Prayer can be requests, and requests can be selfish. Now we know that the Lord wants us to pray; he says that we have not because we ask not. Prayer is pouring out our heart, it is saying to the Lord, 'Lord, I

24

need so and so. Lord, I am in trouble.' This is prayer. But intercession is never to do with myself. Intercession is standing in the presence of the Lord for his interests and his purpose and his burden. That is ministry to the Lord, and the highest dimension in prayer.

When we learn to read the mind of God and are identified with his will and his heart, and when we stand with him in the secret place against all the powers of darkness and evil for the fulfilment of his purpose and will, that is ministry to the Lord, and that is what Samuel did.

All the way through his ministry and his life, Samuel was disappointed and disillusioned. He was disappointed with the people of God, disappointed with Eli, disappointed with Eli's sons, disappointed with his own sons, disappointed with Saul, and if he had lived long enough he would have been disappointed with poor David. I think what David did with Uriah the Hittite and Bathsheba would have broken Samuel's heart. But he never grieved in a wrong way. He went to the Lord and stood before him and worked for his interests right the way through to the end.

> And Samuel said, Gather all Israel to Mizpeh, and I will pray for you unto the Lord. And they gathered together to Mizpeh. . . . And the children of Israel said to Samuel, Cease not to cry unto the Lord our God for us, that he will save us out of the hand of the Philistines. And Samuel took a sucking lamb, and offered it for a burnt offering wholly unto the Lord: and Samuel cried unto the Lord for Israel; and the Lord heard him. And as Samuel was offering up the burnt offering, the Philistines drew near to battle against Israel: but the Lord thundered with a great thunder on that day upon the Philistines, and discomfited them; and they were smitten before Israel (1 Samuel 7:5–6a, 8–10).

Moreover as for me, God forbid that I should sin against the Lord in ceasing to pray for you: but I will teach you the good and the right way. Only fear the Lord, and serve him in truth with all your heart: for consider how great things he hath done for you (1 Samuel 12:7, 23–24).

It repenteth me that I have set up Saul to be king: for he is turned back from following me, and hath not performed my commandments. And it grieved Samuel; and he cried unto the Lord all night (1 Samuel 15:11).

Here you have a picture of a man and the character that God is producing in him. I believe that this prayer life of Samuel's came out of his deep experience of the Lord. That is intercession. You cannot intercede when you are just a babe in Christ because intercession is travail, and travail has to be conceived by the Holy Spirit, and as in the physical realm, you cannot conceive until you are a certain age.

The word intercession is bandied around in Christian circles today, and it often describes anything but real intercession: that comes out of a selfless, sacrificial life with the Lord. It cannot be undertaken if you are self-centred.

In one sense there is nothing more unglamorous, unromantic, and unsensational than intercession. All the other great aspects of service can be seen by other people, but intercession is something which only God sees.

Right from the very beginning, this was true of Samuel. He shines in a way that not even David or Solomon shone. It is almost as if God was saying, 'This is the kind of man that I want for king.' Samuel never actually became king, but he demonstrated real

26

kingship, a kind of spiritual royalty; the character of one who will bring in the kingdom; the character of an overcomer.

Samuel's circuit

Whether we like it or not, we all have circuits. Sometimes we rebel against that: we like to feel that we are special and that we can break out of routine. But the fact remains that every single life has a circuit. The question is, what kind of circuit do you have? Do you have the circuit that involves going round and round in the wilderness for forty years and getting nowhere? Or do you have the circuit that begins at Bethel ('house of God' in Hebrew), and ends in Ramah, the heights of the Lord? Here is Samuel's circuit: Bethel, Gilgal, Mizpah, Ramah.

Bethel

Samuel's circuit began in Bethel, the house of God. That was the one great emphasis in the ministry of Samuel. Everything about him was centred on the house of the Lord. In his day, the house of the Lord was just a tent, and for much of his life, in fact, the ark of the Lord was separated from the tent of meeting. There was disorder and confusion—not at all what God wanted. But the whole of Samuel's life, in those days of disorder and confusion, was lived in the light of building the house of God.

Gilgal

The second emphasis in Samuel's ministry was Gilgal. Gilgal in Hebrew means 'a wheel rolling'. The Lord 'rolled away' the reproach of his people at Gilgal. Do you remember what happened? They took twelve stones from the bed of the river, each one representing one of the tribes of Israel, and they buried them in the River Jordan when it was parted. Then they took twelve stones and put them up in Gilgal. And then the river flowed back. We learn from this that it is not possible to serve God without passing through the crucifixion of the self-life. Then the people were circumcised, and then they kept the Passover.

That is the only way to rest in the Lord. You cannot rest in the Lord if you do not know Jesus as the Lamb of God. You cannot rest in the Lord if you do not know what it is to be justified through the finished work of the Lord Jesus; if you do not know what it is to have your sins cancelled and blotted out. You cannot rest in the Lord if you have an aggressive, ambitious, jealous self-life. When you know what it is to have been crucified with Christ and alive in him, then you have reached Gilgal.

Mizpah

Mizpah in Hebrew means 'a watchtower'. What does a watchtower represent? It represents intercession, watching. Samuel's whole life was spent watching—watching for the interests of God, watching the movements of the Lord's Spirit, watching for the enemy's tactics, watching out for the strategies of Satan.

Ramah

Ramah means 'the heights'. You can never ascend to the throne of the Lord unless you have the house of the Lord in your heart, unless you know the work of the cross by the Spirit of the Lord and unless you

28

know something of real intercession and ministry to the Lord.

Here then is the life of Samuel. May God make us Samuels.

2
Saul

2

Saul

THE MAN OF FLESH

We turn now to consider now that unbelievably complex character, King Saul. I imagine that many people have real sympathy for Saul. When we study this man's life, it is not so black and white that we can easily judge him as utterly evil, wicked, godless or without the Lord. It is not as simple as that.

I believe that the most important lesson we can learn through Saul is this: a person can be saved, can have a great knowledge of the Bible and the things of God, can do great work for God, and yet miss out on the building of the house of the Lord. There may be great devotion in that person, there may be much sacrifice, there may be much knowledge, but also within may be the seeds of destruction. Within our very life, within our character, there are the seeds that can lead to us being diverted from the purpose of God.

The story of Saul is not a fairy story. Wherever we look today in the work of the Lord, we see those who began with the Spirit and have ended in the flesh; those who had a real anointing but somehow or other have fallen; those who have had revelation given to them of the purposes of God and have ended up not building the kingdom of God but building their own empire. And if we look within ourselves we will discover—perhaps on

33

a smaller scale—the very same character faults that shut Saul out from bringing in the kingdom of God.

Saul came to the kingdom and sat on the throne. He was anointed with the same holy oil with which David was anointed. We are not dealing here with an unsaved man. We are dealing with a man who was a child of God. We are dealing with someone who belonged to God's covenant people. He was circumcised as David was circumcised. He was a member of one of the twelve tribes of Israel as David was. Yet, in spite of the fact of being in the kingdom, he could not stay on the throne. He had the kind of character that God had to veto. God has to ban that kind of character from coming to the throne, or every kind of confusion and division and vile deed will come into the kingdom of God. The lesson we can learn from the life of Saul is of tremendous importance. It is true we shall be looking at the negative and not the positive, but we need to do it. It is an uncomfortable picture that we shall be looking at here; uncomfortable because it comes so close to home.

Mere flesh cannot inherit the kingdom of God

The first thing I want to underline is very simple: mere flesh cannot inherit the kingdom of God. It may be noble flesh—decent, gifted, talented flesh, but it cannot inherit the kingdom of God. It may have about it much that is good, but it cannot inherit the kingdom of God; it cannot reach God's goal. It has within it a bias. I do not know if you know that ancient game of bowls—not the ten-pin bowling type, but the old game which Francis Drake played when the Armada arrived. This type of bowl has within it a bias. It does not matter how straight you throw it, it goes off at an angle; and this is a picture of the carnal Christian. He has within him a bias. It does not matter how much it looks as if he will hit the goal, he cannot because of the bias in him that takes him off course.

The man of flesh cannot sit with Christ on the throne. It is impossible. He may want to obey God, but he cannot. He may want to be devoted to the Lord, he may want to give himself unconditionally to the Lord, but he cannot. He finds within him—in his very nature—a power endemic and pathological which prevents him from giving himself to the Lord. He can use all the right words, but almost as soon as the word is out of his lips, he has to serve self. He may recognise the mind of the Lord, but when it comes to practical situations, he does what the world does.

Now I don't know about you, but this is me. We can have a great respect for the word of God and for his law, a real recognition of divine principles, but when it comes to actual practical situations we do what the world does. We fall back into what all unsaved people do in the end. This is the man of flesh. And that is the story of Saul.

Outwardly magnificent

Saul was head and shoulders above other men. He was magnificent to look at. He was a man's man—the kind of man the whole world could respect and go after (1 Samuel 9:2). Outwardly Saul was endowed physically with everything that one could associate with royalty.

35

Caring and thoughtful

Saul was not some delinquent. He was not a rebellious drug addict or alcoholic. This was a man prepared to go out searching for his father's asses. Now I live just a few miles from where all this happened; and I have walked up the hills and I have driven through the valleys. The whole land of Benjamin is a land of deep ravines and gorges and high mountains, and it is impossible territory. And yet this young man went out looking for those wretched asses, even though he came from a good family. He could easily have said, 'Dad can buy another bunch of asses,' but he went out and searched. He was not some delinquent playboy. He was caring and he was thoughtful.

Naturally humble

He was also humble. In 1 Samuel 9:21 we read:

> And Saul answered and said, Am not I a Benjamite, of the smallest of the tribes of Israel? and my family the least of all the families of the tribe of Benjamin? wherefore then speakest thou so to me?

> Therefore they inquired of the Lord further, if the man should yet come thither. And the Lord answered, Behold, he hath hid himself among the stuff (1 Samuel 10:22).

That is amazing. This fellow who was head and shoulders above all the rest was so humble that he ran away and hid himself among the baggage. This was the great baggage that goes on the camels, so by crouching down behind it he could hide himself completely for a while. This is not the picture people usually have of Saul. They think of someone arrogant, presumptuous,

36

big-headed, his pride as big as his height. But this is not the Saul we see here. Here we see him not only thoughtful and caring and responsible, but also with a modest side to his personality.

Magnanimous

When Saul was chosen to be king, a whole lot of the young fellows who knew him said: 'We will not have him. We will not respect him. We will not obey him.' When the children of Israel heard that the Philistines were coming against them, it says that they quaked and trembled at the news. But Saul said, 'Don't fear; the Lord is with us.' And he went out against them, and a tremendous victory was given to Israel. Then the whole of Israel said, 'Bring out those base fellows who said they would not obey Saul, and we will execute everyone of them in front of him.' Now you might think Saul would have liked that. After all, this is the man who flung a javelin at David. We can imagine him saying, 'I want those fellows out of the way altogether.' But no. 'And Saul said, There shall not a man be put to death this day; for today the Lord hath wrought salvation in Israel' (1 Samuel 11:12–13).

Are you beginning to get another picture of Saul? Let's go a bit further.

Spiritually gifted

Saul was not only thoughtful and responsible, not only modest, not only magnanimous in his dealing with those who had antagonised him or stood against him; he was spiritually gifted. This man went among the prophets and prophesied, and so came the saying into

37

Israel which is with us to this day in Hebrew: 'Is Saul among the prophets?' The Spirit of the Lord came upon him and he prophesied.

Now some people put a lot of emphasis on prophecy. They feel that if you can only prophesy, you've arrived. But as I always say, Balaam's ass prophesied. It is not really so amazing. If an ass can prophesy, so can you and so can I. And so could Saul. He lay all day on his face before the Lord. He was spiritually gifted.

He recognised what is of the Lord

Saul recognised that Samuel was truly of God and when Samuel turned to leave on one occasion saying, 'God has finished with you,' Saul took hold of Samuel's garment and tore it. He wanted to hold him, he wanted to keep him. And later still he got a medium to bring Samuel up from the dead.

Why was there such jealousy within Saul's heart of David? Surely it was because he recognised in David a man after God's own heart; someone in a different dimension to himself.

So we can see that Saul was not gross, sensual, and without spiritual gifts or graces. That is not the picture of him we see in the Scriptures.

He honoured God's word

There is one last thing before we finish this. At times, Saul honoured God's word. Look at the amazing story in 1 Samuel 14:3–35. Jonathan had gone out and won a great battle, but it was reported to Saul that the people were eating flesh with blood in it. And Saul was angry. He immediately went out to stop them. How interesting that a man who broke so many other laws of God should care so much about this one. He was a real mixture, and that is why we cannot say he was all bad. He wasn't. There was a tremendous amount about him that was good and noble and spiritual. Yet, this man did not come to the throne of God.

The outward appearance

The carnal Christian or the man of flesh places all the emphasis on outward appearances and talents and not on heart and character. You only have to have a few signs and wonders, a miracle or two, some power, and everybody looks at that. Now I am all for the acts of the Lord. As far as I am concerned, the more signs and wonders we have, the more evidence of the presence of the Lord, the more marvellous it is. I do not believe, as some do, that all these things have passed away. No, whenever the Spirit of the Lord has moved in the whole history of the church, there have been signs and wonders, evidence that God is present. I am all for the acts of the Lord; but I believe we also need to understand the ways of the Lord.

The man of flesh always stops at appearances. That is why he can be deceived and led astray or diverted from God's purpose. People come to me again and again and say, 'How is it that we got into this muddle? How did we get deceived? How did we get led astray?' The reason is that we look at appearances. Sometimes things can appear biblical; they can seem very spiritual. Sometimes they are actual acts of the Lord, but we fail to see beyond them.

Short cuts

The carnal Christian, the man or woman of the flesh, cannot wait for the Lord. This is the problem. They have to have instant churches, instant empires, instant hierarchies, instant elderships, instant diaconates, instant apostolates, instant prophetic orders. They have got to have the whole thing sorted out in a few days or a few months. They cannot wait for the Holy Spirit to work organically to produce things. Instead they have to rush in where angels fear to tread. So we have every conceivable New Testament pattern of church in existence. It seems as if every conceivable experiment that could have ever been made in church life has taken place somewhere. There has not been any of that waiting, like the apostle Paul waited for elders to develop, for the gifted ones to be made manifest and the local assemblies to see it. He may have known, but he waited for the Spirit of the Lord, not only to bring them to the right place, but for those local fellowships to recognise those people who were the Lord's choice.

The man of flesh loves short cuts. He wants to get to holiness in an instant. He wants to get to maturity by a short cut. He wants to bypass the suffering and get into the prosperity. He wants to come to the end—fulness, power, glory—without the cross, without dying. This is the man of flesh.

You will see this principle illustrated everywhere. But you do not have to look at others, for you will find the same capacity within your own heart. We want short cuts, we want everything instant, just like instant coffee, instant tea, instant whipped cream. When we come into the Christian realm, we try to apply the whole instant mentality there. It is amazing how often we rely on man's schemes, man's techniques, man's methodology, the way of the world—the right thing done the wrong way. This is the man of the flesh.

Look at 1 Samuel 15. Here we find the story of Saul being told by the Lord through Samuel that he must wait for Samuel to come. But as he waited, the people began to get nervous. It was pre-battle nerves and they said, 'We have got to get on with it. Where is Samuel? Why doesn't he come?' They could not find Samuel anywhere, and they began to drift away. They hid themselves in caves and holes and they ran away in fear. Finally, Saul said, 'I will do it.' And he sacrificed the sacrifices. Almost immediately, Samuel appeared.

Now there is a kind of patience which is not patience. There are people who never get round to doing anything. They never take a step forward, never pioneer anything and are never prepared to move forward. They may tell us they are being patient, but it is not patience at all; it is unbelief. We are not talking about that. That is not patience. Real patience is when a man of action is kept waiting for the Lord; when a person who is positive and active has to wait for the Lord. That is the test of spiritual character. Can they wait on the Lord and can they wait for the Lord?

Consecrated flesh

The man of flesh always wants to keep what is good in his flesh. This is true of all of us; we cannot help it. We sort through ourselves and our characters and personalities and we think: 'That is bad; the Lord must deal with that. That is ignoble; the Lord must deal with that. That is base; the Lord must deal with that. But *that* is talented; I will devote that to the Lord. That is gifted; I will devote that to the Lord. That is noble; I will give that to the Lord.' We get this idea that all the bad things in our flesh must be put to death, but all the good things in our flesh can be sanctified and consecrated to the service of God.

My dear child of God, *the church of God and the work of the Lord have suffered far more from consecrated flesh than base and ignoble flesh.* I have known people who have had such an organising talent that they could organise the Holy Spirit out of any work of the Lord in just one month. 'This gift of organisation, this gift of administration is not from the pit,' they say. 'This is a marvellous God-given gift. I will devote it to the Lord.' But let them loose in the work of the Lord and you have killed the work of the Spirit.

Now I know this raises problems. What do we do with those who have a musical gift? Do we destroy it? What do we do with those who have a gift of singing or a gift of speaking? The Lord may or may not use those gifts, but if he does use them, it will be because they have come through the death and burial and resurrection of Jesus. Only when they have come through that process can God fill them with his glory and his power. Only then will people no longer hear or see you—they will see and hear the Lord.

> And Samuel came to Saul: and Saul said unto him, Blessed be thou of the Lord: I have performed the commandment of the Lord (1 Samuel 15:13).

Saul really believed he had done what the Lord commanded. He had put to death all the blemished, all the diseased, all the ugly, and he had kept the best to be consecrated to the Lord. Samuel asked one question:

'What meaneth then this bleating of the sheep . . . ?' It is a good question. I think there is a lot of 'bleating' in many of our lives. The man of flesh always tries to use his best gifts and his best energies for the Lord, but he finds that within him there is a poison, there is a deviant, and with the best intentions in the world he cannot go straight.

Do you remember our Lord's word when he began to speak about going to the cross? Peter said to him, 'Lord, you cannot do that. Never, Lord, never. We will not allow it to happen.' And the Lord turned, looked into his eyes and said, 'Get behind me, Satan.'

Now if you came to me with a question about something and said, 'No, I don't think that is the right way. Really I don't,' and I turned around and looked into your eyes and said, 'Get behind me, Satan,' you wouldn't like that. It is one thing for me to say to you, 'Listen, I think you are thinking negatively,' or 'I think you are perhaps subject to some demonic activity or some sort of dark force that is manipulating you and the way you are thinking.' That doesn't sound too bad. But if I were to say, 'Get behind me, Satan,' you would respond, 'That is the most terrible thing I have ever heard in my life. You called me Satan. How can you call a child of God Satan?'

But Jesus called Peter Satan. What did he mean? He meant simply this: your best intentions, your best talents, your best energies, the most noble part of your flesh has within it a ground for Satan. It will never allow the full will of God to be done in your life or in the lives of others. It will not go to the cross. Immediately after Jesus had said these words to Peter he brought the disciples and the multitudes together. Then he said: 'Whosoever will come after me, let him deny himself, and take up his cross, and follow me. For whosoever will save his life shall lose it; but whosoever shall lose his life for my sake and the gospel's, the same shall save it' (see Mark 8:33–35).

We are dealing here with something that lies at the very heart of the whole work of God and of what the Lord calls spiritual, Christ-like character. It is not the consecration of your old nature, however talented, however decent, however energetic it is for God. That is not what the Lord wants. In the final analysis, uncrucified flesh cannot obey the Lord. It can go so far but in the final analysis it cannot go through with it. There is a deviant in us; there is a bias that takes us off course. We cannot face the totality of the cross and the work of the Spirit.

Everywhere I go I hear people speaking about the baptism of the Spirit, the power of the Spirit, the anointing of the Spirit. Now I believe in such an experience, but why doesn't anyone talk about the baptism of the Holy Spirit *and of fire*? When the Holy Spirit comes upon a person, he will burn up the dross. He will take us as a whole burnt offering for the Lord: not just the bad, but every part of us is to go on the altar, and out of the ashes will come a new life. That is regeneration. The altar of burnt offering spells total, absolute death to all that we are. But this is too much for us. And it was too much for Saul.

Do you now begin to understand Saul? Do you begin to understand how like us he is and how like him we are? If you don't remember anything else from the story of Saul, remember this: *in the final analysis the carnal Christian cannot obey God.*

44

Undealt-with flesh invites demonic activity

An uncrucified self-life, however noble, however gifted, however talented will always be ground for demonic activity. That is why you can begin with the Lord and end with the flesh; you can begin with the Spirit and end in destruction. All around us we can see men with real anointing, with real gifts, who have fallen in one way or another, or built enormous empires for themselves. They have become slaves to funding instead of bondslaves of the Lord Jesus. Some people would say this is just the flesh. I hope that it is, but I have to tell you that when Saul was not prepared for the absolute and total work of the Spirit of the Lord, an evil spirit came upon him, and into his heart came a jealousy that was never there before. He could not control himself. This noble, magnanimous, modest man, this man who could recognise the things of God, took a javelin and flung it at David. At one point he was so mad that he would have killed even his own son, Jonathan. Here was a man who had repented before God two or three times, but who had never really allowed the Lord to deal with him, and in the end, he went to consult a witch (see 1 Samuel 28).

What did Jesus mean when he said to Peter, 'Get thee behind me, Satan'? What did James mean when he said, 'This wisdom . . . is earthly, sensual, devilish' (James 3:15)? Sometimes we have taken the meaning out of that word 'devilish', so that we speak of it as meaning horrific, or unpleasant. But the word actually means that demons are involved. The wisdom which is *not* from above, the wisdom of this world, which most of us use and which is the common wisdom in our church affairs and in the work of the Lord, can sometimes have demonic activity in it. Is there any wonder then that there are factions, divisions, jealousies, rival and gossip among us?

Manipulation

The man of flesh is jealous of his position, jealous of his work, jealous of his influence. He always feels threatened. He can never spontaneously, honestly and genuinely recognise the work of God and go along with it. He always feels that somehow he is threatened by another person's gift, position or influence. The New Testament speaks a lot about the works of the flesh and the wisdom which is from this world. It is full of jealousy and strife.

Are not our fellowships so often filled with jealousy and strife? And are they not sometimes wrecked because we feel threatened by another person's gift, by the possibility that one of those other brothers or sisters may have a more powerful influence, a more spiritual gift than we have? We can't help it, but eventually this kind of thing leads to manipulation. When we feel threatened by someone, we start to manipulate things so that they cannot have too much influence or too much power. And manipulation is a form of witchcraft.

The thing we call gossip is often just nothing other than assassination. Now none of us would go so far as to assassinate one another physically, but many of us are involved in the assassination of another person's character. At the root of that spirit of assassination, that spirit of gossip, is fear of another person's gift and influence.

46

Playing the fool

Before we turn to something more positive, there is one last lesson from this picture of Saul. The man of flesh always ends in the same way. These were the words of Saul towards the end: 'I have played the fool, and have erred exceedingly' (1 Samuel 26:21b). What a tragedy to come to the end of our physical life as believers down here and have to say, 'I played the fool and erred exceedingly. I just play acted all the way through and there was nothing real, nothing genuine in my life. I have carried it all through with outward appearance, with a projected image of spirituality, with my natural gifts and talents. I have played the fool. I have erred exceedingly.'

Saul died by his own hand, and so do all men of the flesh. Maybe not always by physically ending their life, but those who sow to the flesh will reap corruption unto death. It is as if you had taken a sword and, like Saul, slain yourself with it. Listen to the words of Jesus: 'For whosoever will save his life shall lose it; but whosoever shall lose his life for my sake and the gospel's, the same shall save it' (Mark 8:33–35).

There is no more real way of committing a kind of suicide than by being a man or woman of the flesh.

God's answer

Poor Saul. Whenever I have spoken on Saul, I always have a number of people come up to me afterwards and say, 'I feel so sorry for him.' The Lord will do the right thing by Saul in the end, but the fact remains, his story is there as a warning. It is no good just feeling sorry for Saul. Do you see something of him in

47

yourself? Are you going to end the same way? Or are you going to let the warning of the Lord come to you and challenge you, so that for the first time you wake up to the possibility that you might be a Saul and might end the same way—a reject from the throne?

The absolute lordship of Jesus

The answer is to recognise the absolute lordship of Jesus in your life. I do not mean calling him Lord but not doing the things he says. I mean what it says in 1 Corinthians 12: saying that Jesus is Lord by the Holy Spirit, so that it is genuine and shows that you are ready at whatever cost to follow the Lord. If he says stop you will stop. If he says go you will go. If he says wait you will wait. You are going to be under the absolute lordship of Jesus.

Let me put it another way: if you and I do not want to end up the same way as Saul and be a reject from the throne of God, we must learn the lesson of utter obedience. At the very heart of Saul's experience are these words: 'To obey is better than sacrifice' (1 Samuel 15:22). Are you ready to be obedient? Maybe you are fearful of what it might mean for your life. I do not want to take away that fear because if I were to belittle that fear in you there would be no faith. It is that fear of what the Lord might require of you, that fear of the unknown, that fear of committing your life out of your hands into his hands that makes you trust him. You can never obey him if you do not first trust him. Believing in the Lord is not quite the same as trusting the Lord. If you trust him, then you will obey him. And if you obey him, you will find in

48

the end nothing to be ashamed of, nothing to regret, only cause to praise the Lord.

I don't know why this is so hard for us. 'Oh dear,' we say, 'I wish he had not brought this matter up because I just know that if I start to really obey the Lord, I mean deeply, truly, totally obey the Lord, I am going to have to be a monk or a nun. That is what is required of me. This is the way it is going to be.' My dear friends, whatever the Lord requires of you, it is for your good. You have got to trust him.

The sentence of death

What is the cost of obedience? 'Deny yourself, take up your cross, and follow me.' That is the cost. It will not come down. There is no cheap way, no short cut. That is the only way you can follow the Lord and become a disciple. The only way.

And the Holy Spirit is the only one who can enable us to do these things. It is interesting that the apostle Paul said, 'Through the Spirit . . . mortify the deeds of the body' (see Romans 8:13). Nobody can ever overcome this deepest instinct in us all to glorify ourselves, to fulfil ourselves, to express ourselves, to make way for ourselves, to assert ourselves. We cannot help it, it is natural. Only when the Spirit of the Lord is in a person and upon a person can that person, for the first time, do the impossible. I say it is impossible to take up your cross and follow the Lord. Of course, there are people who try, and it is then that we get all this unbelievable, artificial piety—everything is dark and heavy. When they sing, it is like a funeral march. That is the cross for some people. Actually, it is religion, not the cross at all. But when the Spirit of the Lord comes upon you, he enables you for the first time to give up all rights to yourself, to take up your cross, and follow Jesus.

We have the benefit of hindsight here. We understand that Jesus was talking, as it were, from Calvary. But when the disciples first heard Jesus say these words about taking up a cross, it was stunning. Every one of them had seen a very common sight. In the crowded streets and bazaars of Jerusalem there would be a sudden commotion and people would be pushed out of the way by some soldiers. Suddenly, a slave would appear with a great placard on which was written the person's crime, and then coming up just behind was the person himself with the crossbeam. The criminal would carry that crossbeam on his shoulders to the place of execution and his hands would be nailed to the crossbeam. It was hauled up into place and, finally, the feet were nailed to the vertical post.

So what did they understand by these words? They understood one thing clearly: that person carrying the crossbeam was not yet dead but the sentence of death had already been pronounced. He had no more rights. He was on his way to execution.

My dear friends, you and I have been crucified with Christ. We cannot crucify ourselves. In fact, all we can do is accept the sentence of death from God. That means we give up rights. We say, 'I am a dead person; I have no more rights.' And thereafter it is for the Lord to arrange our circumstances, situations and relationships. At work, at home, in our fellowship. He arranges them beautifully—and they will crucify you. Within hours, certainly within days. Once you have accepted the sentence of death, once you have seen that with Christ you have been crucified and you accept that sentence of death within yourself, then for the first time, the Lord can deliver you from being a man or woman of flesh. He can transform you. There is no need for us to end like Saul. We can end like Samuel, or David, or Solomon. Will you be a Saul or will you be a Samuel? Will you be a Saul or will you be a David? The choice is yours.

3
David

3

David

THE MAN AFTER GOD'S HEART

We come now to look at the character of David. His name has become a household word, and when we consider David, we consider that which is of God. We actually think of the Lord Jesus—David's greater Son. David's influence is amazing—like that of Moses or Abraham. Every child of God has some understanding of David. This is all the more interesting because in some ways David actually fell more deeply than Saul. That is why I suppose some Christians have such a great sympathy for Saul. They feel that what happened to Saul was almost unjust because David did something that even Saul did not do. He arranged for a very faithful man of God to be left alone in the front line of the battle so that he would be killed. And David did it because he wanted that man's wife. It is a terrible story, the story of David and Bathsheba. Saul never fell as deeply, yet Saul is rejected from the throne and David's throne is established.

Even more remarkable is the fact that, once David confessed his sin and returned to the Lord, the Lord made Bathsheba the mother of the two men who are in the Messianic line—Solomon and Nathan—instead of the son of David's first wife or Abigail. This terrible sin, once it was confessed, was woven by the Lord into his purpose. And it leaves us with an enormous problem because we wonder why the Lord dealt so drastically with Saul and so mercifully with David.

Then David did another thing that was a sin. He had been told specifically that he should not number the people. All the nations around Israel numbered their population so that they could boast over who had the greatest population, who had the greatest birth rate, who had more men than women, and so on. David had been told that he must not number the people, but he numbered them—and then a plague began. He saw the angel of the Lord standing with his sword over Jerusalem, and he realised that he had sinned before the Lord. The amazing thing is that when he confessed his sin, he discovered the place where the temple should be built. That angel stood over the threshing floor of Araunah, the Jebusite. In that moment, David discovered, through his sin, the place where God was going to build his house.

What is David's secret? How is it that he can fall and be restored and his very sins be woven into the purpose of God? As you look at the story, you almost wonder if the Lord predestined those sins. The Lord must have known that Bathsheba was going to be the mother of Solomon and Nathan. You have one genealogy in Matthew and another in Luke—one through Nathan and the other through Solomon—and both of them are of the Messianic pedigree. How incredible. It almost makes us wonder: can we sin that grace may abound? Of course not! But why does the Lord reject Saul, who had so many good qualities, who right to the end of his life was always vacillating, being sorry and saying the most wonderful things? He said to David: 'Now I see that you will be king and that your kingdom will be established for ever.' Yet Saul was rejected. Saul died by his own sword with only a depressive word on his lips. David died with his lips speaking of the Messiah who was to come.

If we can discover David's secret, it can change our whole lives. It can bring us to an understanding of the grace of God and of the kind of character which goes right through to the throne. Not one of us is perfect. Some of us think we are, especially when we are younger, but if we live long enough we discover that even the most noble and decent among us is not perfect. We are all capable of the grossest and most depraved sins, but with the Lord there is mercy. Where there is genuine repentance and a heart for the Lord and a desire for absolute sincerity, then the Lord can do so much.

Direct experience of the Lord

David steps into history with the story of Goliath. We, of course, know of the secret visit of Samuel to Jesse, and how Samuel already knew that the Lord had rejected Saul and had said that one of Jesse's sons was going to be the king whom God longed for and desired. But actually, David only became publicly known and recognised with the story of Goliath. In that marvellous story of David and Goliath in 1 Samuel 17 we discover something about David. This victory that David had over Goliath was not some sudden heroic gesture, some sudden emotional surge. It was the outcome of something that had already happened in the young David's heart.

'Who is this uncircumcised Philistine, that he should defy the armies of the living God?' questions David.

Now isn't it strange that Saul did not have these words on his lips? Isn't it strange that David's brothers—all of them magnificent—did not have these words on their lips? Isn't it interesting that in the whole army of Israel, all mobilised, all brought there for war with the Philistines, not a single one had this attitude or this spirit? But David already had an understanding of the God of Israel. He had his own revelation. He had his own experience from within his own circumstances and his own situation. He was only a shepherd lad at that time, being the youngest of his brothers.

Even today in Israel you can see all around little boys sitting out there looking after sheep and goats. I took a group about six weeks ago out by one of the wadis, the place where Elijah was fed by the ravens. As we walked along the path with a great drop down one side, there was a little lad on the other side of the ravine with about three hundred sheep and goats. He sat on a rock and played a little homemade flute, and he entranced them with his melodies. When his goats got out of hand, he stood up and said something, not in Arabic or in Hebrew, but in goat language. It was quite extraordinary. All the goats stood still, and then he threw some stones. Suddenly, the intransigent ones ran back into the herd. The people I was with were so fascinated by this little boy they forgot me altogether, and nearly fell over the edge in their delight.

David was the youngest, and that is the job of the youngest. The youngest is always the most insignificant. It is the firstborn who is the most important. Everything is for the firstborn. He is Mother's favourite, Father's favourite, everybody's favourite. All the brothers are in awe of him; he is the firstborn. And the youngest, especially when he comes at the end of a large family, well, there is nothing but the sheep and goats for him.

So here was David out in the valleys. He could have become bitter, or developed an inferiority complex. He could have felt he was overlooked, and become filled with anger towards his brothers or his father and mother. But no. David worshipped the Lord. Some of his loveliest early psalms (if we accept Jewish tradition) come from his youth when he was out there with those sheep and goats in the wadis, the hills, the mountains and valleys of Judea and Benjamin. Out there, alone with his sheep and goats, David had his own experience of the Lord.

When Saul said: 'You are just a boy, not even in your late teens. How can you go against Goliath?', David replied (and I paraphrase): 'Let me tell you, your majesty. When I was keeping my sheep and goats in the wilderness, a lion came and took one of the lambs in its mouth. I went after that lion and took the lamb out of its mouth, and I took the lion by its beard and took its head off. Also a bear came after the sheep and I did exactly the same. It was because the enemy [if we were to put it in New Testament language] was robbing me of what was my responsibility. He was damaging the flock, spoiling that which was my responsibility. Who is this uncircumcised Philistine that he should defy the armies of the living God? I will do the same thing with him.' I think Saul must have gulped a bit. This was unbelievable.

I think if I met a lion I would fly. The nearest I have been to such an experience was when a huge, great old boar, a male pig, charged me. I have never been so frightened in all my life. It was all very well for the brother with me, who was a very phlegmatic individual, to say, 'Stand still, stand still, and when he comes near you, jump to one side.'

The lad David could easily have said, 'I have all these sheep, what is one lamb? It is one meal. Dad won't worry about that; he would rather have me alive.' But there was something about David. It was not just pride, arrogance or presumption; he had an experience of the Lord, and by the Lord, he did it. He had a responsibility and he felt that he needed to rely on the Lord to discharge that responsibility; so when those enemies came and sought to take away that which belonged to him, that for which he was accountable, then he trusted the Lord and slew those enemies in the name of the Lord. Indeed David had his own direct experience of the Lord.

Our tradition tells us that the twenty-third Psalm was written when David was in his teens. And because of the simplicity of this beautiful little psalm, it is probably more familiar than any other. But it reveals an experience. Here is a teenager speaking. He had a lot more experience yet to come, but the fact is, from the very beginning, this man had his own personal, direct experience of the Lord. Why do we so often think that you can only have experience of the Lord when you get into ministry or become a missionary? Why do some people think that only if you are in Christian work can you have direct experience of the Lord? My dear friend, your kitchen can be the place where you have direct experience of the Lord. You can have direct experience of the Lord in your business or in your family. It is the way you look at it. Do you look upon your family or your business as something given you by God, a responsibility that you are accountable for? However young you are, do you trust the Lord for that responsibility to give good account in the end for what he has entrusted to you, even in the most simple things?

Right from the very beginning, David understood something about the house of the Lord. One of our traditions suggests that David's mother was a weaver of the tabernacle veil. In the Talmud the story goes that David, as a little boy, watched her with some of the other women weaving that huge veil for the tabernacle. When he asked her what it was for, she told him that the veil was for the tabernacle, but that the tabernacle of the Lord was all separated and in a mess. There was no permanent place for the Lord to dwell.

We don't know whether this is a true story or not, but something must have happened to David very early on, because he says, 'Surely goodness and mercy shall follow me all the days of my life: and *I will dwell in the house of the Lord for ever.*' What is he talking about? He is not a priest, nor is he from the Levitical tribe. Why is he talking about dwelling in the house of the Lord for ever? Could it be that somehow something had dawned upon him concerning the purpose of God to have a place where the Lord's name would dwell, that would represent the Lord, and where his glory would be expressed?

Let's look at another instance of this matter of direct experience of the Lord: David refused to wear Saul's armour. I love this part of the story of David and Goliath. Here is this great huge six-foot-five fellow, with massive shoulders, looking down upon David—who was an athletic boy, but certainly not six foot five. He was apparently the shortest of the family, but he was good looking. And it is a very beautiful thing that it says in Hebrew, 'He had fair eyes.' You could see something in David's eyes. We always say the eye is the window of the soul. There was something inside that shone out of David's eyes, and people noticed it.

Saul looked at this boy standing before him, and he said: 'Now listen, you cannot go out against that great giant. His spear is like a weaver's beam. You will just be dog's meat. So I am going to dress you up. Come here. Bring my armour! Come here, David. Put my armour on him.'

They began to put the heavy mail upon David, clunk, clunk, clunk. They put the sheaves on his legs and shod his feet. They put the plate across his breast, and then they gave him the great sword in one hand—and David couldn't move! I can just see David trying to lift up his feet, and saying, 'Sir, I can't go out in this.' And Saul, of course, must have looked down through the head-piece and seen David somewhere down below and said, 'Take it off.'

Then David took his own sling, his own pouch, his own staff, and he selected his own five pebbles. What is the Lord saying? *It is better to go out with what is ours than what is somebody else's.* If all our Christian life and work is spent trying to get into somebody else's armour, it is so silly. In the end, you can only work with what the Lord has given you and done with you and what he has taught you to use. This was David's experience. He had no experience of Saul's sword or Saul's javelin. He did not know how to hold Saul's shield. Maybe in time he would be able to, but at that point he could not use any of it. But he had very real experience with those stones and with his catapult. These were things he had sat for hours using.

The best way for shepherds to get those goats is with a sling and a small stone. They just pick it up and sling it, and you will see a goat right at the front jump and run back into the herd. David knew how to use a sling and pebbles. He had to use them every day. They were his normal weapons, the tools of his trade. He was used to these things. Doesn't this teach you and me something? We all try to imitate people we think are great in the Lord. We should certainly imitate their faith and their devotion, but you have to be you and I have to be me. We have to be ourselves in the Lord, and we have to have our own experience of the Lord.

A man after God's own heart

A man after God's own heart is a person, however poor, however young, who has his own direct, personal experience of the Lord Jesus. He has his own experience and revelation of the Lord. It is not second hand.

Look at David's psalms. Have we anywhere in the whole word of God anything like David's songs? They are written over his whole life from his youth to his old age, and they give the most amazing revelation of experience. When you are in trouble, is there anybody else who speaks to you like David? Maybe it is because I am Jewish, but I find that David speaks to me in a way that nobody else speaks. I understand David. I read the Psalms when I am in trouble, and I always find the Lord gives me something from David.

This man had such an amazing experience of the Lord. He learned things that believers under the New Covenant do not seem to learn. He learned how to praise the Lord in dark days. He learned how to overcome through worship. He learned how to go forward in faith. He learned that you have to be absolutely real when you have sinned. You have to call it by its name and face it in all its ugliness and ask the Lord to create in you a new heart. His was not a second-hand experience. He didn't study the life of Abraham and then write all these psalms based on Abraham's experience, or on Moses' experience. Of course he quotes Moses and Abraham, but it is his own experience of the Lord. Here is a man after God's own heart. Here is the character that comes to the throne. It is not a character that cannot fall. It is not a character that does not have passions just like you and I do. It is not a character that cannot get horribly enmeshed in evil. It is a character that wants the Lord and wants him first hand.

Fighting the Lord's battles

This man after God's own heart fights God's own battles. Now this is a very important thing, and I want to be very clear on this. I go all around the world and to be perfectly honest, I have to tell you that most Christians are fighting their own battles. Everywhere I go, I see fellowships and assemblies in confusion and division and faction. People are fighting battles, but they are not the Lord's battles. Mostly they are battles which arise out of jealousy, rivalry and ambition. People try to make it all spiritual, but it is not spiritual at all. It is the character of Saul all over again. Even where there is nobility, decency or a magnanimous nature, it is the character of Saul. It cannot come to the throne; it cannot stay on the throne. David didn't fight his own battles, he fought God's battles.

In one sense, we could say that the lion and the bear were David's battles. The whole great fulfilment of God's purpose did not hang on that lion and that bear (or perhaps they did?). But that was the kindergarten school, and before long, we find that David is fighting battle after battle. What Joshua and the children of Israel never dealt with, David, by the Spirit of the Lord, deals with. Joshua, for instance, was never able to take Jerusalem. They said it was too strong. They said there were iron chariots. They said they could not do it; it was a Jebusite stronghold. All they had to do was put their feet down. That is all the Lord said: 'Wheresoever you put the sole of your feet, I will give it to you.' But they said they couldn't do it; it was impossible. It was invincible. And so it was left for hundreds of years, until David's men put their feet down on the water shaft that went up within the walls of the Jebusite stronghold and, in that moment, it fell to the Lord. It was the Lord's battle. This Jerusalem, which the Lord had chosen for the place where his name was to dwell, David took. And then all the Girgashites, the Hivites, the Amorites, the Amalekites and all the other 'ites' that Joshua should have dealt with, David took, one after the other. I know some Christians get very upset about all this slaughter, but these were God's battles.

David's faith expressed in the battle with Goliath gives us the key to all the other battles he fought. Look at what David said to Goliath publicly. It would have been one thing to say it privately, but David proclaimed it publicly:

> This day will the Lord deliver thee into my hand; and I will smite thee, and take thy head from thee; and I will give the carcases of the host of the Philistines this day unto the fowls of the air, and to the wild beasts of the earth; that all the earth may know that there is a God in Israel. And all this assembly shall know that the Lord saveth not with sword and spear: for the battle is the Lord's, and he will give you into our hands (1 Samuel 17:46–47).

Now this is a youth speaking. He is not even in his late teens, and here he is speaking out publicly. All those other children of Israel should have been ashamed. They were adults, some of them battle-trained, and not one of them had this kind of faith. And what faith it is! 'This is the Lord's battle,' says David. He did not see it as an avenue for him to come to prominence and catch the public eye. He did not even see it as a means to ministry, as if he was going to be something among those people of God. He was just so absolutely shattered that no one could see that this great Philistine had challenged the Lord. 'And if this Philistine has·challenged the Lord, the Lord will take him on, and if no one else will be with the Lord in this, I am going to be with him.'

When you and I have our battles with one another in the work of the Lord or in the fellowship that we represent, the Lord leaves us to it. The more we fight and squabble, the more we try to put one another down and devalue one another, the more the Lord just says: 'Get on with it. If you want to fight like that you can do it.' But it is a different thing altogether when we fight the Lord's battle. Then we don't have to fight for our reputation or our ministry; we don't have to fight for our status or any position of glory. All we have to do is stand out of the way and let whoever is the enemy collide with the Lord. It is so simple.

All David did was to say: 'Goliath, you have taken on the Lord. If you think you can defy the Lord and frustrate the purpose of God and enslave God's free people, you have another think coming. The Lord will make mincemeat of you.' And the Lord made mincemeat of him. It is unbelievable. That great lumbering giant came out with his weaver's beam. He could have

66

dropped it on David and it would have crushed him. He could have bashed him with it and it would have finished David. He said, 'Am I a dog that you come out to me with a staff and a pouch and a catapult?' And David slung one stone. Isn't that amazing? People have often asked me why he selected five stones when he only needed one. I suppose the others were insurance. I don't know. But I think it's great that he only needed one small stone. Can you imagine it! If I had had you all there watching this great battle, and I took this little pebble and put it here, and I took this great javelin and put it here, and I took this little catapult and put it here, and then I put this great big shield of Goliath's here, you would have said, 'This is presumption; this is ridiculous.' But David had learned the lesson: don't fight your own battles, fight God's battles.

Paul makes the same point in the New Testament in 1 Timothy 6:12: 'Fight the good fight of faith, lay hold on eternal life, whereunto thou art also called.' Here again is the fight that is the Lord's fight, not ours. God means you to have life and more life. He wants you to be an overcomer. He wants you to be a good soldier of the Lord Jesus, but you cannot become a soldier if you are fighting your own battles with other believers or with your unsaved boss or unsaved relatives. That is not the Lord's battle.

Later on in 2 Samuel 8, we have a whole list of all the enemies of God's people subdued, one after the other. When you get a person with his own experience of the Lord and who fights God's battles, it becomes infectious. Before long, others who have an experience of the Lord and who want to fight God's battles will join you. And so we find all David's mighty men gathered together. For a long time they were in a cave called

Adullam. This is a most amazing cave; I have been in it. It is a huge labyrinth cave in one of the great wadis that goes down to the Dead Sea. We know it is that cave because it is the only cave that has a spring of fresh water in it. Otherwise, you could not possibly keep 400 men in a cave with all their families and everything else.

I remember when I was first saved and I did not know anything about the Bible, there was an old lady in the fellowship and she was always praying in the prayer meeting about 'the cave of Adullam'. I could not think what was going on in Adullam's Cave because she was always saying: 'And all these people are in the cave of Adullam, Lord. We are in that cave of Adullam with you.' It stuck in my mind long before I even knew the Bible. I finally found out that it was the cave of Adullam where these people had gathered to David. They were all in debt, all in trouble, all of them restless because they felt things were not going right in the nation. And God was training them into a marvellous spiritual commando force that was to spearhead the way for the whole nation.

When David finally died, after his last words we have a whole record of all the mighty men—how this one did this, how that one did that. These were mighty men who had the same direct experience of the Lord, the same experience of faith, and were fighting the same battle of the Lord's.

Waiting for the Lord

The third thing we learn about this man after God's own heart is the exact opposite of Saul. He is a man who waits for the Lord. I cannot emphasise this enough. The man who is a man after God's own heart will wait for the Lord and will not move until the Lord moves him, until he gets his direction. David's character was produced through this waiting for the Lord. David had the opportunity to shorten this waiting period, not once, but again and again and again. But he learned to wait. He knew he could shorten it with the arm of the flesh, and that is what Saul always did. But David learned it was no good if he did it with the arm of flesh; the result would be trouble and division and faction. There would be no glory.

Waiting was not easy. Don't think that David just went off to some palace with great gardens where he could shut the iron gates, go in and lie down on some silken bed in an air conditioned room and have the most wonderful time while servants waited upon him. Oh no. Waiting for the Lord meant that David was hounded from pillar to post. He had to sleep out in the wild in the rough, sometimes up in the mountains, sometimes in holes of the earth, sometimes in wadis. We believe that the great crag that today we call the Masada, which means 'fortress' or 'stronghold', is the one mentioned where it says, 'David got up into the stronghold.' It is the one great crag that is invincible, and it is right near to Engedi where some of these other things took place.

It is interesting that David's experience ranged over a whole area that was about eighty miles by about thirty miles. Now to those of us with cars, that is nothing. But for David and his men it was an enormous area to be hounded over. If you were harried day and night and you knew someone was hunting you like an animal and meant to kill you, what would you do if suddenly he fell into your hands? Don't you think you would say, 'Oh, Lord, thank you.' Now this happened two or three times for David, but the two really big accounts were when, as the Scripture puts it very discreetly, 'Saul went into a cave to cover his feet'. It meant he went to relieve himself. And while he was in there, with his clothes outside, David came. And David's men said: 'The Lord has given him into your hands; he is trapped. He is in the cave. He has got to come out, he is naked. We will have him. He is mincemeat just like Goliath.' And David said: 'You do not lay a hand on him. He is the Lord's anointed. It is not the Lord's time' (see 1 Samuel 24).

Then another time Saul went to sleep with his spear next to him, his chief of staff, Abner, by his side and his great standards at his head. David's men crept up close to him. 'Let me do it,' said Abishai. 'I can do it in one blow. He won't even know what hit him. I will put a javelin right through him and pin him to the ground and that will be the end. Then we can go home and live like human beings instead of being hunted like wild animals.' And David said: 'Don't do it! Don't touch the Lord's anointed' (see 1 Samuel 26:7–9).

The whole of Christendom is filled with people who cannot wait. They have always got to get to the top. They want the platform ministry, the leadership; they want to be apostles or prophets or pastors or teachers. They get jealous and full of ambition and they put others down. They cannot wait for the Lord.

If some of you are troubled because people are speaking against you and disparaging you and devaluing you and saying you are nothing and all the rest of it—let them. Suffer it. Wait for the Lord. Don't fight back. It is a good thing to bear the yoke in your youth. It is a good thing to be disparaged and devalued sometimes so that you learn the lesson of waiting.

Nobody will ever come to the throne of God and reign with Christ who does not know what it is to wait for the Lord. Sometimes this will involve you in very much suffering, but it is truly the fellowship of his suffering. It will be a time when you go down into the depths, when you are broken. It will be a time when you feel as if you are in poverty. But if you shorten that time, be sure you will not come to the throne. There is no short cut. This is the Lord's discipline. Actually, we learn more when we wait for the Lord than in any other situation.

For David it never ended. The Lord brought him to the throne: first he was crowned king of Hebron or Judah, then, seven and a half years later he was crowned king of all Israel. You would have thought that now all the problems are past; now he is in the place to which he was called and for which Samuel anointed him. But he doesn't go very far before his own son, Absalom, the one he loved more than all his other sons, the one who was so magnificent to look at, so athletic, so gifted, led a rebellion against him. It broke David's heart. And the great and mighty men of David, especially that hard man who was David's chief of staff, Joab, said, 'Let us kill him.' But David said, 'No, this is the Lord.' And David went out as a refugee. You remember how Shimei cursed him as he went out and someone said, 'Let me kill him.' And David said: 'No, it is the Lord. Let him curse.'

David not only waited for the Lord and never grasped that throne, but when he was there, he learned to let it go when the challenge was made. No wonder he came back to it, and no wonder God said, 'I will establish his throne for ever.' And no wonder the Lord revealed to him that there would come One of his seed of the tribe of Judah, of the house of David that would sit upon his throne and reign for ever. I think David must have died with the most marvellous sense of fulfilment. Even if he knew that his sons would go off the rails, yet there was going to come One of his seed in the end who would sit upon that throne for ever.

Centred in God's purpose

That leads me to the last thing I want to say. This man after God's own heart is a man whose own heart and life are centred in God's purpose. Whatever is on God's heart is on this one's heart. This is the most marvellous thing about David. He so wanted to build this house of the Lord, almost as if he felt it was the meaning of his life, and perhaps the greatest cross that ever came to him was when the Lord said, 'You shall not build it.' David could have retraced his steps and said, 'Why has the Lord done this to me? Why?' He could have gone under a cloud of disillusionment and disappointment. He could have been offended with the Lord. You know, many believers get offended with the Lord. I hear it all the time. They come to me and say, 'Why did the Lord do this?'

But not David. David said: 'Very well, the Lord will not let me build this house, but I will put aside all the gold, all the silver, all the wood, all the materials, and I will store them. I will go through the whole area and collect everything I can, and I will get it all ready for my son to build this house.' No wonder David, at the end of his life, could truly say, 'Surely goodness and mercy will follow me all the days of my life, and I will dwell in the house of the Lord for ever.'

If you want to know the heart of David, read Psalm 27:

> The Lord is my light and my salvation; whom shall I fear? the Lord is the strength of my life; of whom shall I be afraid? When the wicked, even mine enemies and my foes, came upon me to eat up my flesh, they stumbled and fell. Though an host should encamp against me, my heart shall not fear: though war should rise against me, in this will I be confident. One thing have I desired of the Lord, that will I seek after; that I may dwell in the house of the Lord all the days of my life, to behold the beauty of the Lord, and to inquire in his temple.

He goes on to speak about his father and mother forsaking him and everything else, but then we read, 'When thou saidst, Seek ye my face; my heart said unto thee, Thy face, Lord, will I seek.'

A psalm was written many years later, not by David, but about him:

> Lord, remember David and all his afflictions: How he sware unto the Lord, and vowed unto the mighty God of Jacob: Surely I will not come into the tabernacle of my house, nor go up into my bed; I will not give sleep to mine eyes, or slumber to mine eyelids; Until I find out a place for the Lord, an habitation for the mighty God of Jacob. . . . For the Lord hath chosen Zion; he hath desired it for his habitation. This is my rest for ever: here will I dwell; for I have desired it (Psalm 132:1–5, 13–14).

This man after God's own heart is the man whose whole life is centred in the Lord, and in the purpose and burden of the Lord. Whatever is on the heart of the Lord is on his heart. This is the man whom God seeks after. Do you begin to see the difference between Saul and David? Saul had so much that was noble and decent

73

about him, but he did not do the will of the Lord. He could not wait.

David brought the ark of the Lord home to Jerusalem. He was not permitted to build the house of the Lord, but at least he was able to do one thing. That ark of the Lord, the ark of the covenant, represented the very presence of God. Far more important even than the tent of meeting is that ark of the covenant. David brought it home. He prepared all the materials for the building of the house of the Lord. Yes, David fell, but he also repented. So we leave David, and we leave him with the very last words on his lips which, to me, sum up the whole of his life:

> Now these be the last words of David. David the son of Jesse said, and the man who was raised up on high, the anointed of the God of Jacob, and the sweet psalmist of Israel said, The Spirit of the Lord spake by me, and his word was in my tongue. The God of Israel said, the Rock of Israel spake to me, He that ruleth over men must be just, ruling in the fear of God. And he shall be as the light of the morning, when the sun riseth, even a morning without clouds; as the tender grass springing out of the earth by clear shining after rain. Although my house be not so with God; yet he hath made with me an everlasting covenant, ordered in all things, and sure: for this is all my salvation, and all my desire (2 Samuel 23:1–5).

I think it is the most wonderful grace of God to be given to any servant of the Lord or to any child of God to die with this upon their lips. I imagine that the way you die and the very last things you say virtually sum up your whole life. Then whatever it is that was the burden of your life will finally come out when you have very little time left. And so it was with David. He died talking about Jesus. In one sense, his whole life had been

74

wrapped up with the Lord Jesus and the fulfilment of God's purpose to bring a Messiah. The whole story, even the temple of the Lord, the obtaining of Jerusalem, the pacifying of the land, all had to do with the coming of Messiah. And now when he dies, he looks forward to the Lord Jesus.

Do you want to be a Saul or a David? And if you want to be a David, I have another question. Are you prepared for the cost? There is a price attached to this following of the Lord and being of this kind of character. May God give us the grace to say, 'Lord, I will follow you whatever the cost.'

4
Solomon

4

Solomon

THE SERVANT OF THE LORD

Believers are very divided on the character of Solomon. There are those, especially among Christians with Gentile backgrounds, who find Solomon a great embarrassment. They do not understand why the word of God says how wonderful he was and how he fulfilled the purpose of God. All they can see are his many faults. Then there was a whole teaching a century or two ago, but which has gone out of fashion these days, that the Lord never meant there to be a temple, that it was all a terrible mistake. The Lord meant there to be a tabernacle that was a kind of prefabricated building that could be put together, because the people of God were really only sojourning on this earth.

When we look at Chronicles, the Scripture does not say anything about Solomon's faults; it just refers to his wives. But the record in Kings is very, very honest about what happened to Solomon. So I want you first and foremost to understand that Solomon finished what God began with Samuel and continued with David. In one sense, Solomon is the final act in this fulfilling of God's purpose concerning his people. Solomon sums up all the lessons that we have learned. We find in him Samuel's life summed up, Saul's tragedy summed up, and David's life and character summed up. So, in one sense, he completes the whole picture for us.

A servant

Solomon teaches us that the character God is looking for in the person who comes to the throne, who will build his house and see and experience the glory of the Lord filling everything, must supremely be a servant. No matter what happened to Solomon later, we see into the heart of a character that God desires to produce in every child of God in the amazing response that Solomon spontaneously gave to the Lord.

One of the best ways to test a person is to give him a dream. When the Lord comes to you in a dream, you do not have anything ready so that you can be artificial, or think of the right thing to say. You are forced to be quite spontaneous. The Lord came to Solomon in a dream and said to him, 'Ask what I shall give thee' (1 Kings 3:5). Now Solomon could have asked all kinds of things. He could have said: 'Lord, I need the wherewithal to absolutely dazzle the heathen nations around me. I want you to give me such splendour and such prosperity and such blessing that Egypt will be knocked over, and Babylon and Syria flattened. Now of course, Lord, it will be all your glory. But I want you to do something that will make this throne that you have brought me to and this kingdom that you have established to be absolutely sensational as a testimony.'

Or he could have said: 'Now, Lord, I want you to destroy all these enemies. Just let them die, drop dead. Let them have strokes, heart attacks, cancer, a few other things, Lord. It's up to you how you do it. Just let them be removed, all of them. I don't want to have a kind of

Marxist purge of all these unpleasant elements in the court and around me. You know, Lord, there are all kinds of people plotting. Would you just take it into your own hands and wipe them out one by one? Then we can get on with serving your interest.'

No. Solomon said: 'Lord, you were very good to my father, and one of the greatest goodnesses that you have expressed to my father is to cause one of his poor sons to sit on the throne in his place. But I am very young and I am very inexperienced. I just do not know how to go out and come in [meaning into the presence of the Lord, as well as before the people]. I do not know how to deport myself. I do not understand everything. How can I actually glorify you? I need a wise and an understanding heart so that I can administer justice for these people, discern between good and evil, and be able to rule or judge this great people that you have chosen.'

This is not the kind of royalty that most of us imagine royalty to be. Maybe we still have the idea that a king sits there dressed in marvellous robes with a great crown on his head and an enormous orb in one hand and a sceptre in the other. He sits there waiting to be admired, dripping with diamonds and jewels. We do not understand that real kingship is a matter of service.

When we come to the biblical ideal of kingship, we see it, of course, in Jesus who came to be the bondslave of all. This is God's King. There was not a drop of anything but royal blood in the veins of Jesus, and yet he was a servant from beginning to end. It was his Father's business he was about. Even the night before he was betrayed, he washed the feet of his disciples saying he was leaving them an example. This is kingship. Now this is entirely foreign to most of us because our whole concept of coming to the throne is of authority and power and being able to throw one's weight around and having lots of people running at our beck and call. We do not understand that kingship is to serve.

But we see it in Solomon right at the beginning of his reign. When he was still young, we see a character of service. Character is *never* produced or matured or developed by self-pleasing, self-worship or self-aggrandisement. Service is only produced when we are prepared to lay down our lives. Solomon served the Lord, and he became the builder of the house of the Lord. Whatever faults and failings he had, the one thing he did was that which had been on the heart of the Lord from the beginning; he actually built the house of the Lord.

The rest of the Lord

Nathan the prophet gave Solomon a name when he was born. It was Jedidiah, which in Hebrew means 'beloved of the Lord', just as David means 'beloved'. But David called him Solomon, and this means 'peace'. It comes from the word *Shalom*, 'peaceful', or 'his peace'. David was not allowed to build the house of the Lord because he was a man of war, and the Lord said, 'You shall have a son and he shall be a man of peace, and he shall build the house of the Lord.'

In Hebrews 4 we read of the Sabbath rest, which means that we have ceased from our own strivings and from our own works and entered into the rest of the Lord. Wherever I go, people who begin to get the truth into their heads and not their hearts start fighting. There is unrest and confusion and division and factions. This one wants this and that one wants the other.

Wherever I go, I see the brothers charging one another like bulls. And this is supposed to be the house of the Lord. What in the world is wrong with us? Is the house of the Lord just to be a place where everyone has got to reach their own fulfilled ambition? Is it to be a place where everyone has got to become a powerful elder or minister of the word? Why can't men die to self? Why can't we fall into the ground and die, so that out of the ashes the Holy Spirit can produce the body of the Lord Jesus? But no, we fight and fight.

In Europe or Britain you get to be somebody if you have the right blood, the right connections, or you went to the right school. In America success is the dream. Anyone can reach the top through sheer ability. But all this can become a curse to us when we enter the kingdom. We still retain that self-centred, egotistical drive to be something in the house of the Lord, to grasp the ministries, to use the gifts, to reach the top. We strive to be a success in the eyes of our family and in the eyes of our brothers and sisters.

When the Lord came to Solomon, he could have just said: 'Lord, give me success. I need success. There is nothing like success to breed success. If all my enemies see that I am a success, they will be silenced. All my brothers of the royal blood will not try and take the throne from me if they see that I am a success.' But all he asked for was that he might be given a wise and understanding heart that he might go in and out before the Lord and before the people. That is service.

Even if you feel uncomfortable with Solomon because of certain aspects of his lifestyle, please get this lesson. His name means 'peace', and the house of the Lord is never built through fighting. It is never built by falling into factions and fighting things out with one

83

another. It is done by falling into the ground and dying. Then, even if everybody else has ambition, something has happened in you.

I tell you, there is nothing like the rest that comes as a result of being freed from this drive for success. When you have died to your own ambitions and your own reputation, your own gift and your own ministry, then you are free to be the servant of the Lord. What does it matter if people walk over you? What does it matter if people take away your reputation?

There was a godly old brother who was tremendously used of the Lord in Scandinavia in the early part of this century. His name was Fjord Christensen. He was an old Lutheran Danish pastor. Wherever I went in Scandinavia, years ago, people used to tell me, 'Do you know what pastor Christensen said when I went up to him after a meeting and said, "Your talk was too long"? He opened his wallet and took out a silver piece and said: "I must give this to you. I have promised the Lord I will pay everybody who keeps me humble."' I don't know how much money he spent, but he always gave something to anyone who criticised him or took away his reputation, because he said they were doing him such a service.

There is something in us that cannot bear criticism. We cannot bear having our reputation taken away; or to be made into a doormat. But look at it like this: only the Lord can bring you to the throne. Your brothers and sisters cannot put you on the throne, nor can you put yourself on the throne; only the Lord can bring you there. And if you will only let the Lord do his work and produce in you the character of sacrificial service, you will become a man of peace.

It takes two for division. Have you ever thought

about that? If one person will not allow it to happen, it is not really a division. It is only a sort of rebellion. But if you come against me and I come against you, and you start spitting fury at me and I start spitting back, then we have a division. Supposing when you come at me and you spit fury and I just allow you to do it. Then it is not a division any more. And I tell you something else very interesting: the Lord will take you on, and your spitting of fury will be the Lord's business.

No man or woman has that 'peace which passes understanding' unless they know something of the self-life being dealt with. You cannot know the peace of the Lord in all its fulness until you have entered into his Sabbath rest. Now if you do not understand what that means, just ask the Lord to reveal it to you in his own good time—he will.

A hearing heart

Our English Bible translates 1 Kings 3:12 as 'I have given thee a wise and an understanding heart', but in the Hebrew, it is 'a hearing heart'. That doesn't just mean a heart that can hear; and that is why the English has 'understanding' . The idea is that you will never have understanding if you do not hear the Lord. The basis of all wisdom is to be instructed by the Lord. The Lord wants to instruct, but if we do not hear him, we will never get wisdom.

Wisdom and knowledge

The same event told in 2 Chronicles 1 records that Solomon asked for wisdom and knowledge. Knowledge is to do with facts; wisdom is what to do with the facts. Many years ago, when I was living in England, we had a magnificent fuchsia bush. It was one of those standard bushes for those of you who are gardeners. It was a very old plant with a large trunk, and it was in a marvellous antique pot. It stood outside my study window so I saw it all the time. One year, it came out in all its leaves, then all its buds came out, and then suddenly all the buds fell off and lay around in a great thick carpet. I said to the sister who looked after the house, 'Someone has collided with that bush.'

'Oh no, I don't think so.'

'Yes,' I said, 'nothing else would shake off all those blossoms like that.' Then all the blooms came again a week or two later and the same thing happened again. In our fellowship then we had two of the leading botanists in Britain—one of them was one of the top eight botanists in the world and a very godly man. I asked him if he could come and look at the fuchsia bush. He bent down and looked at the bush. He plucked a leaf off and held it up to the light. Then he scratched the bark. He parted the earth and looked at one of the roots, and then he gave me an amazing dissertation on the pedigree of this fuchsia bush. He told me of the two different species that had been crossbred, one from Brazil and one from somewhere else, and he gave me all the Latin names. I stood there with my mouth open and a kind of glazed look in my eyes. Finally he named three possible diseases that might have caused the blossoms to fall.

'So what should we do?' I asked. He looked at me totally blankly and said, 'I don't really know.'

So I thought I would try the other younger man who was also a top botanist. He came and went through the same motions. He plucked a leaf off and scratched the stem. He didn't give me quite such a long dissertation, but he told me it could be this or it could be that.

'What should we do?' I asked, and he too looked at me blankly.

These men had knowledge; they knew all the facts. They knew what kind of fuchsia bush this was, how it was a hybrid. They had the whole history of its background, but they could not tell me what to do.

Just above us there was a market garden, and in it was a dear old man who became the basis for a whole radio series that is still going on today, thirty years later. His name was Dan Archer and he had a real country brogue. I went to him and said, 'Dan, could you come and look at the fuchsia bush? Something is wrong with it.'

He did the same as the others. He looked at the leaves. He scratched the stem. And then he said, 'You know what this bush needs?'

'No,' I replied.

'It needs a good dose of Epsom salts.'

Now Epsom salts were sold all over Britain for 'inner cleanliness'. I thought he was trying to be funny, so I laughed at him.

'I am not joking,' he said. 'Go down to the chemist and get some Epsom salts and give it one tablespoonful a day.'

'Dan,' I said, 'do you want me to be the laughing-stock of the whole fellowship? If they find out I am giving a tablespoonful of Epsom salts to a fuchsia bush, they will laugh themselves silly.'

'Well,' he said, 'if you want the thing to die don't do it, but it will recover in no time if you do as I say.'

I couldn't do it. I thought someone would be bound to look out of the window and see me. So I said to one of the sisters, 'I want you to go and get some Epsom salts and put one tablespoonful on this bush each day.' And she went and did it. She was a very humble person. Within two weeks the bush had recovered. Now that is the difference between knowledge and wisdom. How we need knowledge *and* wisdom!

Many Christians do not understand what is happening in the world. They do not understand where we are in the purpose of God. They don't even have knowledge. They are just at sea. Sometimes when things happen in our families or our fellowships, we do not understand them.

God revealed to Solomon that the house of God was an absolutely central fact to the purpose of God being fulfilled. When you hear Solomon's marvellous prayer in 1 Kings 8, you realise that he understood, he had the facts. Only God could have revealed to him that the Lord wanted that temple to be built so that his name could dwell there.

But more than that, he had wisdom. He could apply those facts. There are so few people who know how to apply the facts, and so we play at churches. I go sometimes to places where people are quite clear on certain things to do with the church, but there is no life. It is almost as if the truth of the church has become the central foundation upon which they meet, and not the Lord.

The whole world came to hear Solomon because God gave him such wisdom. It is said of him that there was nothing to do with trees or birds or animals or plants that he could not talk about. He created three thousand proverbs, of which we have a selection in the book of Proverbs. This Solomon, if we believe tradition, is the one who wrote Ecclesiastes, and therein is revealed the wisdom that, without the Lord and an understanding of his purposes, all is vanity. You might as well eat and drink and be merry because tomorrow you are going to die anyway. There is no great point to living. Do not be too righteous and do not be too bad because you are going to die anyway. Everything is useless.

But when we come to the Song of Solomon, which tradition also tells us was revealed to Solomon in a dream, we come face to face with a burden on the heart of God. This is not some bawdy little love ditty as the liberal theologians would have us believe. It is not a collection of love songs based on Syrian customs. Jewish tradition tells us that God revealed in an allegory the love in his heart for his own bride and the union and communion he desires with his people. And suddenly, it is no longer all vanity. The whole of life and all its circumstances and situations is suddenly related to the purposes of the Lord. There is something the Lord wants to do with us, something he wants to do in us. It is no longer emptiness, it is fulness. It is no longer purposeless, but purposeful. That is why I always tell people never to study the little book of Ecclesiastes without the Song of Solomon; they are meant to go together.

I want to come back again to this matter of a hearing heart. Don't you think this is our problem? How few leaders there are who hear the Lord. It is not how many faults you have or how many weaknesses you have. I wish that my faults or weaknesses would be cut right down, not just to a minimum, but to nothing, and I wish the same for you. But I want to tell you something quite shocking. If I had to choose between a leader who has weaknesses and faults and who hears the Lord and a leader who does not have so many weaknesses and faults but does not hear the Lord, I will choose a leader who hears the Lord every time. And that is the way the Lord dealt with Solomon—and with David before him. It is the way he dealt with Saul, because Saul, with so many good characteristics, could not hear the Lord. He bent everything to his own self-fulfilment. He took short cuts even though he was warned not to take them. This is the lesson that comes home to us. Do we have a hearing heart?

My Auntie Dagmar used to give me some money at the end of every Sabbath (Saturday) if I could quote without mistake a whole portion from the word of God. So I used to learn a chunk every week. I was always full of questions about what I had learned: 'What does that mean, Auntie?' And she would explain it to me, and I would say, 'I cannot understand it, explain it to me more.'

In the end, she said to me, 'In James 1:5 it says that if any man lacks wisdom, let him ask of God who gives to all men liberally and upbraideth not, and it shall be given him if he ask in faith nothing wavering. Now,' she said, 'I want to know from you, do you or do you not lack wisdom?'

'Yes, I lack wisdom,' I replied.

'So, we have got down to a good basis. If you lack wisdom you can ask the Lord on the basis of this scripture, and he gives it and does not argue. He does not upbraid. He will give it to you.'

Her words sank into my heart, and from that moment, I began to ask the Lord every day, for many years, every time I got on my knees, 'Lord, I do not have any wisdom. Please give me wisdom.' Now I had never read my Bible until I was twelve years of age. I had never been in a place of worship. I had no knowledge. I used to say at school that I thought Jesus was a myth. I did not think he even existed. I thought those terrible Christians had made up this person. But I can say that I found that the Lord kept his word: he gave me under-standing. I believe he can give it to anybody who will ask.

This matter of hearing is so important I cannot over-emphasise it. To hear the Lord is the heart of all God's training, all God's education and instruction.

The still small voice

I want to give you another illustration from life of one of the greatest characters in the Old Testament, Elijah. How God used Elijah in prayer! How God used him as a testimony! When he said, 'The heavens shall not rain for three years,' it did not rain for three years. And then he told the king, 'It will rain.' The heavens were like bronze, but he got on his knees and he prayed and prayed until the rain came.

You know the story of Elijah on Mount Carmel with all the prophets of Baal. He took on the whole array of evil in the land single-handed and represented, as it were, the Lord. But Elijah had a lesson to learn.

After the great triumph on Carmel, and after the rains came in answer to prayer, Jezebel wrote Elijah a note: 'God help me if I do not do to you by this time tomorrow what you have done to my prophets.' And without waiting to ask the Lord about it, without giving the Lord even a chance to speak to him, Elijah fled for his life. He ran out of Galilee through Samaria to Jerusalem into the Negev and flung himself under the juniper tree and said, 'Lord, let me die.'

The Lord said, 'What shall I do now? I really should talk with him. But he is in such a state I cannot.' So the

Lord said to the angels, 'Go and cook him breakfast.' The angels cooked him a breakfast and Elijah ate it, but he was so worn out he said, 'I just want to die.' He slept the whole day because you do not travel in that part of the world by foot during the day. He slept the whole day under the shade of the juniper tree, and then the angels came again and they shook him and said, 'Supper.' And in the strength of that food, he went forty days and forty nights in the wrong direction. Isn't the Lord amazing? Sometimes he helps us go in the wrong direction. Don't think that if angels appear to you and minister to you that it means you are going in the right direction. No, the angels were helping him because the Lord was going to catch him at the other end.

When he finally got to the other end, he went up to Mount Horeb and the Lord said, 'What are you doing here, Elijah?' Now for the first time, the Lord could talk to him.

'Lord, you know I am the only one left. They have killed them all, and now they want my life.'

Then the Lord said, 'Stand back,' and suddenly there was a tremendous wind that smote the mountain and all the rocks fell down.

Elijah loved every minute of it. 'Oh,' he said, 'Lord, that was wonderful.'

Then the Lord said, 'Wait,' and there was an earthquake and the whole place shook.

'Marvellous, Lord. What a show!'

And the Lord said, 'Wait.' Then a fire came and burned everything through the mountain.

'Oh Lord, this is so wonderful.'

Then there was a stillness and a still, small voice, and when Elijah heard that voice, he collapsed in a heap. He wrapped his mantle around his head and bowed down and he said, 'Lord, I am no good.'

Elijah was stubborn. He went through the whole excuse all over again: 'Lord, they killed all those people and now they are going to try and kill me.'

But what the Lord was saying was this: 'Elijah, why did you come here? Who told you to come here? You have got to hear me. You mustn't just panic.'

Sometimes when we panic, God has to go with us in the panic because there is no way he can get through to us. He cooks us meals and helps us go in the wrong direction because only when we are a little calmer can he say, 'Let's get this sorted out.' That was the greatest lesson Elijah ever learned. You might summarise Elijah's ministry as earthquake, wind and fire. You could almost say these were the elements, the symbols of his ministry. And there are many people who seem to think that is what ministry is all about: earthquake, wind and fire. Well, thank God, there are outward signs and wonders, but if we do not hear the still small voice of the Lord, they don't mean a thing.

The house of God

The last thing I want to mention is that Solomon is the one who built the house of the Lord. That is the heart of everything, and Solomon understood it. We read in his prayer how the Lord, from the very beginning, had desired this and how he had brought his people out of Egypt for this very reason. That was the explanation of their history, their election and their destiny. Only by wisdom could he have had such understanding.

There are few Christians who understand that the spiritual house God is building is the explanation of

93

our history, our election and our destiny. So few understand it, yet it is everywhere in the New Testament.
This is the character God looks for, a builder of the
house of the Lord, because when we build the house of
the Lord, the glory of the Lord can fill it. Now it is true
that to some extent the whole earth is filled with the
glory of the Lord, but the house of the Lord is something special. The house of the Lord is where his glory
dwells.

The warning

Solomon compromised. One has to have some sympathy with him. He wanted to make peace with all the
nations around him, and the way it was done in those
days was to marry the princesses of the royal families of
the nations. So the first person he married was Phar-
aoh's daughter. She was not a believer. She did not
belong to God's covenant people. In fact, he did not
even want her to live in the palace that was near to the
house of God because he said it was holy, and he built
another palace for her.

But even more sad, once he had married these ladies,
part of the agreement was that they should be allowed
to have their own shrine and worship their own gods. So
Solomon allowed a certain hill just outside of the old
city, the continuation of the Mount of Olives, to be the
place where all these wives could have their shrines.
The word of God tells us of Chemosh, the god of the
Moabites, and Molech, the god of the Ammonites and
the Ashtoreth, the goddess of the Phoenicians. Terrible
gods, who demanded that the firstborn child had to be
thrown into the flames.

Here is this man whom God loved so much, this man

whom God brought to the throne, this man who wanted only to serve the Lord, who longed to be at peace so that he could build the house of the Lord, this man who had a hearing heart, and suddenly, we find him compromising with those who worshipped other gods. Here is a warning to all of us. We are never safe until we come finally into the presence of the Lord. All the way through our lives, we have to be alert and watchful because the devil is going around like a roaring lion seeking whom he may devour. This is not said to make you afraid. It is to make you realise your only safety is in the Lord. You can build the house of the Lord and still somehow compromise. May God help us. May he give us a heart like David and a heart like Solomon. Christian theology believes that Solomon died a backslider, but Jewish theology says that Solomon in his last years returned to the Lord, and that it was in those years that he compiled the Proverbs. One day we shall meet him and know the truth. What I pray for all of us is that we should reach the purposes God has for us without being diverted and turned aside. Only the Lord can do that.

May the Lord give us grace so that we may know his working in our circumstances and situations; in our family life, in our business life, in our church life. May the Lord work to produce character in us, the kind of character that will come to the throne and that will reign with the Lord Jesus. May he produce a character in us that means we can build the house of the Lord.